# PASTOR-PARISH RELATIONS

## Supporting your pastor, staff, and congregation

*By Betsey Heavner*
*General Board of Discipleship*

# PASTOR-PARISH RELATIONS

*Copyright © 2004 by Cokesbury*

*This book is printed on acid-free paper.*

**ISBN 0-687-00060-2**

MANUFACTURED IN THE UNITED STATES OF AMERICA

# CONTENTS

# Our Identity, Call, and Mission

You are so important to the life of the Christian church! You have consented to be among a great and long line of people who have shared the faith and led others in the work of Jesus Christ. We have the church only because over the millennia people like you have caught the vision of God's kingdom and have claimed a place in the faith community to extend God's love to others. You have been called and have committed your unique passions, gifts, and abilities in a position of leadership, and this guide will help you understand some of the elements of that ministry and how it fits within the mission of your church and of The United Methodist Church.

"The mission of the Church is to make disciples of Jesus Christ. Local churches provide the most significant arena through which disciple-making occurs" (*The Book of Discipline of The United Methodist Church, 2004*, ¶120). The church is not only local but also global, and it is for everyone. Our church has an organizational structure through which we work, but it is a living organism as well. Each person is called to ministry by virtue of his or her baptism, and that ministry takes place in all aspects of daily life, not just within the walls of the church. Our *Book of Discipline* describes our mission to proclaim the gospel and to welcome people into the body of Christ, to lead people to a commitment to God through Jesus Christ, to nurture them in Christian living by various means of grace, and to send them into the world as agents of Jesus Christ (¶121). Thus, through you—and many other Christians—this very relational mission continues. (The *Discipline* explains the ministry of all Christians and the essence of servant ministry and leadership in ¶¶125–137.)

## Essential Leadership Functions

Five functions of leadership are essential to strengthen and support the ministry of the church: identifying and supporting leaders as spiritual leaders, discovering current reality, naming shared vision, developing action plans, and monitoring the journey. This Guideline will help you identify these elements and set a course for ministry.

### Lead in the Spirit

Each leader is a spiritual leader and has the opportunity to model spiritual maturity and discipline. John Wesley referred to the disciplines that cultivate a relationship with God as the "means of grace" and suggested several means: prayer, Bible study, fasting, public and private worship, Christian conversation, and acts of mercy. Local church leaders are strongly encouraged to identify their own spiritual practices, cultivate new ones as they grow in their own faith, and model and encourage these practices among their ministry team participants.

### Discover Current Reality

"The way things are" is your current reality. How you organize, who does what, how bills get paid and plans get made are all building blocks of your current reality. Spend time with people who have been in this ministry and with your committee members to assess their view of how things are. Use "Christian conversation," one of the means of grace, not only to talk to others openly about their understanding of current reality but also to listen for the voice of God regarding your area of ministry.

### Name Shared Vision

"The way things are" is only a prelude to "the way you want things to be." When the church is truly of God, it is the way God would envision it to be. Spend time with your committee and with other leaders in the church to discern the best and most faithful future you can imagine. How can you together identify your role and place in a faithful community that extends itself in its fourfold mission of reaching out and receiving people in the name of God, relating people to God, nurturing them in Christ and Christian living, and sending them forth as ministers into the world? Examine your committee's role and its place in that big picture and try to see yourselves as God's agents of grace and love.

### Develop Action Plans

How do you get from here (your current reality) to there (your shared vision)? As a leader, one of your tasks is to hold in view both what is and what is hoped for so that you can build bridges to the future. These bridges are the interim goals and the action plans needed to accomplish the goals that will make your vision a reality. Remember that God may open up many (or different) avenues to that future, so be flexible and open to setting new goals and accepting new challenges. Action plans that describe how to meet interim goals should be specific, measurable, and attainable. While it is faithful to allow for the wondrous work of God in setting out bold plans, balance that boldness with realism. You and your committee will find information and tips here on developing and implementing the shared vision, the goals toward that vision, and the specific action plans that will accomplish the goals.

### Monitor the Journey

A fifth responsibility of leaders is to keep an eye on how things are going. Setbacks will surely occur, but effective leaders keep moving toward their envisioned future. Not only will you monitor the progress of your committee's action plans to a faithful future but you will also be called to evaluate them in light of the ministry of the rest of the church. Immerse yourself and your plans in God's love and care. Voices from the congregation (both pro and con) may be the nudging of God to shift direction, rethink or plan, or move ahead boldly and without fear. Faithful leaders are attentive to the discernment of the congregation and to the heart of God in fulfilling the mission of the church.

# The Staff/Pastor-Parish Relations Committee

Y ou have been elected a leader in your church! Christians have learned that effective spiritual leaders follow Jesus' model of servant leadership. During historical times of church growth and revival, spiritual leaders—both lay and clergy—have served together as servants of God. The church is most effective in mission when leaders who are growing in faith come together for a common purpose. *The Staff-Parish Relations Committee is the administrative unit in a local church where staff and congregational interests are integrated to focus on the mission of the church.*

## Clarifying Terms

The "Pastor-Parish Relations Committee (PPRC)" is truly a Staff-Parish Relations Committee (SPRC) because the committee relates to all staff, both bishop-appointed staff and employed staff. *The Book of Discipline of The United Methodist Church* uses both names for this committee to reflect the use of both terms within the various congregations of The United Methodist Church. Throughout this Guideline, we will use S/PPRC to include both forms of common usage.

The S/PPRC has some of the same functions of a personnel office or Human Resources department in other organizations. There are some legal and risk management issues for which the S/PPRC has responsibility. However, church leadership pushes us to focus our attention on God and away from "business as usual." Even in the midst of meetings or crises, the S/PPRC must never forget they are part of the body of Christ, and they must always be aware of the mission of God's church. The S/PPRC operates under God's leadership in the tension between staff and congregational interests, which includes dealing with both the celebrations and disappointments inherent in any human family and church.

*The S/PPRC has primary responsibility to work with staff so that the mission of the church is realized.* The S/PPRC should have a clear understanding of your local church's mission and vision, built upon the mission of the wider Church. Clear understanding of your church and prayerful listening to God's direction will guide both the development of job descriptions and the assessment of staff.

The S/PPRC works with individuals and groups, including:
- the lead pastor
- all ordained leaders—both elders and deacons—appointed by the bishop

- the lay staff
- the congregation (individually and corporately)
- the community outside the walls of your building
- the district superintendent
- the United Methodist conference and general church staff.

Remember that The United Methodist Church has an appointive system rather than a call system for clergy leadership. The S/PPRC consults with its district superintendent about congregational needs. The S/PPRC members must be attuned to the movement of God's Spirit so that they serve as guides, teachers, mentors, managers of conflict, and interpreters of ministry both to staff and the congregation.

Specific tasks for the S/PPRC include:
- explaining the nature and function of ministry to the staff and the congregation
- conferring with the congregation and the staff/pastor about ministry direction
- assessing the ministry of the congregation and the staff/pastor at least annually
- conferring and consulting with the district superintendent
- supporting lifelong learning for all staff (continuing education)
- identifying and supporting individuals from the congregation whom God seems to be calling for ordained ministry.

# The Job of the Chairperson

Federal laws related to church employee relations are summarized and updated at http://www.gbod.org/congregational

### Help for the Job
Your leadership is a partnership with others. People who can help are the district superintendent; annual conference program staff people; ordained and lay leaders in your church; and people in the community outside your church who are skilled in communication, mediation and peacemaking, law, benefit programs, and social needs. Other sources of help are your annual conference board of ordained ministry, the General Board of Discipleship, the General Council on Finance and Administration, and the General Board of Higher Education and Ministry. See the Resources suggested at the back of this Guideline.

## The Task of the Chairperson

- Ask God to increase your understanding of the way your skills will be used as chairperson of the staff/pastor-parish relations committee.

- Read this Guideline thoroughly to understand the responsibility of the S/PPRC and the committee's relationships with other parts of the church system.

- Make an appointment with your pastor(s) and district superintendent to talk about expectations for the S/PPRC. The goal is to build a partnership for working together. (See the checklist below.) Pray together for your congregation and the leadership each of you has.

- Meet with the previous chairperson to learn how the committee worked in the past and to handle any unfinished business. Get copies of job descriptions, policies, and procedures that have guided the committee.

- Become familiar with the *Book of Discipline*. The 2004 edition will guide your work.

### Clarifying Terms

*The Book of Discipline of The United Methodist Church* describes the form of organization and governance of The United Methodist Church. It is revised according to the decisions of each General Conference. In contrast to other books, the *Discipline* is organized by paragraph rather than page, chapter, or section. The paragraphs are numbered consecutively within each chapter or section, but numbers may be skipped between sections to allow for future additions. There is a table of contents and a topical index. The paragraphs in the 200 section relate to the local church and the paragraphs in the 300 section relate to the ministry of the ordained.

- Consult with chairpersons of other committees who relate to staff people. For example, trustees relate to the work of a custodian; the worship committee relates to musicians and worship leaders; the education committee relates to the director of Christian education, director of youth ministry, and daycare teachers. The S/PPRC has responsibility for proper screening, including contacting references and performing background checks on lay employees of the congregation. The S/PPRC should make sure that appropriate groups conduct background checks for volunteer staff, such as children and youth workers (see the resource *Safe Sanctuaries* for guidance).

- Develop a calendar of meetings in consultation with the pastor, other people who will attend, and the church calendar.

- Arrange for training for the committee, especially new members.

### A Checklist for Conversation With Pastor and District Superintendent

_____ What are conference parsonage standards?

_____ What are conference requirements for continuing education and spiritual formation?

_____ How does the S/PPRC recruit, nurture, and support candidates for certification and ordained ministry?

_____ What are conference policies related to sexual harassment and building safe sanctuaries for all people?

_____ What are conference policies for ministerial evaluation?

_____ What conference policies apply to lay employees?

# The Job of the Committee Members

● Read paragraphs of *The Book of Discipline of The United Methodist Church* to learn what is expected of the Staff/Pastor-Parish Relations Committee. See the previous box about using the *Discipline* ("Clarifying Terms").

● Study this Guideline carefully to help you understand how the committee relates to the overall administration of your local church.

● When the committee has made its schedule of meetings , place these dates in your personal calendar. When you cannot attend, notify the chairperson.

### Reflection

*For as in one body we have many members, and not all the members have the same function, so we, who are many, are one body in Christ, and individually we are members one of another. We have gifts that differ according to the grace given to us (Romans 12:4-6a). What implication does this Scripture have for the S/PPRC?*

# Who Is on the S/PPRC?

The Staff/Pastor-Parish Relations Committee members are nominated by the committee on lay leadership and elected by the charge or church conference. The S/PPRC should be the least homogenous group in the church. Each person should represent or relate to various constituencies in the church. *The Book of Discipline* provides for a rotation system to provide continuity on the committee; it requires that at least five and not more than nine members be elected for terms of three years each, in three classes; it specifies that one member must be a young adult and that all members must be professing or associate members of the church or charge. Retiring members (those who have served three years) may not succeed themselves.

The *Discipline* also requires that a lay member of the annual conference be a member of the S/PPRC. No employee of the church or a member of the pastor or staff member's immediate family may serve on the committee, nor may any affiliated ordained clergy persons. S/PPRC members must be laypersons, other than the appointed staff. The S/PPRC of a charge where there is more than one church must have at least one representative from each church. Charges in a cooperative parish shall meet together to consider professional leadership.

The committee is required to meet at least quarterly. It may be called to meet by the bishop, the district superintendent, the pastor, any other person accountable to the committee, or the chairperson of the committee. It may not meet without the knowledge of the pastor or the district superintendent. In addition, the committee shall meet in a closed session, and all information shared in the comittee shall be confidential. When the pastor or any member of the staff who is under consideration is not present and that person's employment is under consideration, that person must be informed prior to the meeting and immediately thereafter be brought into consultation either by the committee or the district superintendent.

# An Overview of a Year

The functions and responsibilities of the S/PPRC continue throughout the year. The following calendar highlights responsibilities for focus during a particular quarter and suggests a flow for the committee work. It is important that the committee always be attentive to God and be flexible in working with people and ministry.

## First Quarter: January-March

1. Provide training or review for all committee members. In reviewing responsibilities, be sure to include a report on the current status of candidates for certified and for ordained ministry recommended by the charge conference. S/PPRC leads the congregation in supporting and encouraging candidates through the years of training and formation for leadership. The Resources section at the end of this booklet suggests help for this task.

**TIP:**
Assign a committee member to be in touch with candidates. Suggest to your education work area (in a large church) or to your district committee on ordained ministry that there could be a one-time class on "Is God Calling You?"

2. Explore the nature and function of the church and ministry. Remember the mission and vision of your congregation. Review job descriptions and jointly negotiate priorities for pastor and staff to align the job descriptions with the needs and hopes of the congregation. Rewrite the job descriptions as necessary. Make plans to inform the congregation about staff responsibilities and inform the congregation whenever there is a change. Consult with the committee on lay leadership about leadership needed to complement the staff's skills, gifts, and assignments. See the Resources section for help with job descriptions.

**TIP:**
Assign committee members to each staff member to build one-on-one relationships. Often it is best for the chairperson of the S/PPRC to build this relationship with the lead pastor. Joys and concerns may be shared with the committee, as appropriate.

## Second Quarter: April-June

1. Begin the assessment/evaluation of ministry areas and staff. The goal of assessment is to improve the ministry of the congregation under the guidance of God. Effective assessment begins with a clear understanding

between the S/PPRC and the staff members about the expectations of the staff members. While this underscores the importance of job descriptions (see first quarter tasks above), effective assessment also calls for building positive relationships and strong communication skills among the people involved. Suggestions for conducting effective assessment are on several of the following pages. Share the outcome of the assessment with the staff members and agree on who will follow up to improve ministry. Decide who else, if anyone, will receive information from individual assessments and how the assessment will be interpreted by your committee. Assessment can be assigned to subcommittees who work with the pastor and staff members to complete the evaluation of their area of ministry. See the Resources list at end of this Guideline for help with assessment tools.

2. Arrange a parsonage tour with the parsonage family and a representative of the board of trustees for inventory, maintenance, and repair. Keep a liaison with the parsonage family to address issues before they become problems.

3. Review your legal responsibilities with employed and appointed staff. Legal responsibilties include both church and state, and federal law for lay and clergy staff. (See Resources.)

# Third Quarter: July-September

1. Review non-salary support for the pastor and staff, such as vacation, business expenses, housing allowance, and professional and continuing education expenses. Make recommendations to the finance committee for adjustments.

2. Review salary-and-benefits packages for the pastor and staff for the coming year and send recommendations to the church council or their consideration. (The S/PPRC may wish to consult with the finance committee to establish those recommendations.)

3. Review continuing education and spiritual formation plans for the coming year with the pastor and staff.

4. Check with the conference board of ordained ministry to identify guides who can lead candidates through the Ministry Inquiry Process.

5. Interview candidates for ordination as deacon or elder using guidelines contained in *The Christian as Minister* (see Resources).

6. Follow up the evaluations of ministry areas and staff. Evaluate the evaluation processes you have used and revise them to improve the church's ministry.

## Fourth Quarter: October-December

1. Compare vision/mission statements, charge conference goals, and job descriptions. Revise job descriptions to align with the mission and goals of the congregation in consultation with the pastor and the employed staff.

2. Evaluate the total work of this committee. Ask for input from the pastor and staff. Search for ways to improve. The committee and staff should agree on what to report to the congregation and to the church council.

# Conducting Meetings

Your time together as a committee will have (or can have) a huge impact on the congregation, on the committee, and on individual and staff members of the church and S/PPRC. It is crucial that the meetings be conducted in an open, supportive, flexible, participative, and trustworthy manner.

## Sample Meeting Agenda

- Prepare by notifying/reminding committee members and staff of the meeting date, time, and place at least a week in advance; by planning the agenda, including worship relevant to the business of the meeting; and by coordinating with others who will make presentations.

- Correct minutes as necessary for approval. It may be helpful to mail the agenda and minutes prior to the meeting.

- Hear reports from liaisons to the pastor/staff. Any reports should be made after prior discussion with the staff members concerned. Staff members should have the opportunity to share recent joys or disappointments, plans that are progressing for the future, and the most pressing concerns.

- Consider how congregation and the pastor/staff can work together to achieve goals for mission and ministry of the congregation.

- Have a time of learning and education for the committee related to its task. (See "Skills for Committee Members.")

- Review the decisions and recommendations made during the meeting and clarify who is responsible for the actions.

- Conclude with a brief evaluation of the meeting. How has the meeting helped to advance the mission and vision of your church? What issues have been raised for future agendas? How have committee members experienced God's love and guidance in this meeting? Spend some time in prayer.

## Your First Meeting

- Open your meeting with worship, seeking God's guidance. Use 1 Corinthians 12:4-13 as a scriptural basis for the committee's work.

- Provide training about the job for new and continuing committee members.

- Study the paragraphs from the *Book of Discipline* that relate to the work of the committee and make plans to carry out those tasks and responsibilities. (See ¶259.2)

- Agree on the procedures for your decision-making and discussions. There are suggestions of procedures in *Behavioral Covenants in Congregations: A Handbook for Honoring Differences* by Rendle (see Resources).

- Stress the absolute necessity for confidentiality as it relates to what goes on in the committee—not only the actions taken, but also the discussions preceding the actions. It is very important to discuss this when you are establishing how you will work together. It is very difficult to introduce this concept when there is tension over an issue. Remember that the administrative task of working with personnel is different than the program ministries of other committees. It is helpful to reflect on the difference between confidentiality (private matters shared in trust) and secrecy (something hidden or concealed).

- Elect a vice-chairperson and a secretary.

- Assess last year's committee activities. Which activities are ongoing? What needs to be added or taken away in order to fulfill the mission of the church? How can the committee work as a team to help the church accomplish its mission?

# Skills for Committee Members

The sample agenda calls for attention to education and training for the committee. Among skills that are useful for the S/PPRC are communication skills, hospitality and celebration skills, and peacemaking and mediation skills.

## Communication Skills: Listening and Responding to the Church and Community

The S/PPRC listens to many different voices. It listens to the congregation, the community, the pastor, the staff, and the people in the United Methodist connection. Some of these voices need help to say what they really want to say, and the S/PPRC may need to ask their opinions in interviews and surveys. The S/PPRC should use active listening skills to make certain different voices are clearly understood.

Body language is an important part of communicating. We often reveal more about what we are thinking by our actions than by our voices. Be alert to what people are saying with their posture, gestures, hands, eyes, heads, arms, and legs.

**Active listening requires the full attention of everyone involved.** Without listening, no communication takes place. Careful listening is such a critical task for the S/PPRC and for the congregation that you might consider arranging training sessions. Resources may be available in your community through sponsors of crisis hot lines or a school's communication department.

### A Checklist for Good Communication

_____ Encourage the other person to stay in the present, the here-and-now. Acknowledge ways that past activities are a strong foundation for current ministry, but stay away from the "we used to do it" scenario.

_____ Begin statements with "I believe," "I feel," and "In my opinion." Encourage others to do the same.

_____ Ask what the other person is feeling, if appropriate. Body language is a clue. Be aware of your own feelings as well.

_____ Repeat what you hear to ensure accuracy. Ask questions for information and clarity.

_____ Build trust by finding what you can agree on, then move on to any differences.

_____ Accept; do not judge. This does not necessarily mean reaching an agreement.

_____ Suggest opportunities for in-depth conversation (at home, on a walk, at lunch, and so forth).

_____ Provide ways people can share new ideas. One congregation supplies pew racks with a card saying, "I wish our congregation would _____."
People are encouraged to submit ideas by filling out a card and putting it in the offering plate.

## Hospitality and Celebration Skills

The S/PPRC is the cheerleading squad for the staff of your church. Hospitality includes a pleasant environment for the staff to work in and the tools and equipment for the job. The S/PPRC leads the congregation in celebrating the work of the staff. Acknowledge specific examples of ways the staff builds the mission and vision of the church.

_The United Methodist Book of Worship_ includes services to celebrate the appointment of clergy leaders and to say farewell to clergy leaders. It is also appropriate to recognize lay staff in worship, especially when praising God for the gifts of staff in leading the congregation. Remember that it is important to acknowledge staff members in addition to the usual times (at the beginning or end of their appointment/employment and at Christmas time).

## Deal With Rumors: Communicate the Facts

When rumors begin to circulate, it is essential to communicate the facts quickly. Rumors begin when people discern a few facts or impressions and then fabricate the rest of the story. The way to stop rumors is to communicate openly and honestly what you know. It is also very important that all members of S/PPRC and church leadership communicate the same message. In order to do this, write a message that everyone can speak about publicly, without speculations or side comments. Stick to the facts and remember your covenant of confidentiality.

If the committee hears a rumor, investigate first to find out the facts. Facts reside not simply in what one person says happened but also in the discerned evaluation of what all parties say happened and the context in which it happened. S/PPRC members must separate emotion and rumor from facts. _When appropriate,_ share facts through a brief notice in the church newsletter or from the pulpit.

Because of the confidential nature of S/PPRC work, avoid using e-mail if possible. E-mail is easily manipulated and can circulate around the world in seconds, so use extreme care if you must use e-mail to address rumor, conflict, or other sensitive matters.

Most importantly, develop a plan! The chairperson and committee members should all be clear about:

- who speaks on behalf of the congregation
- when you involve the district superintendent, bishop, or conference staff
- the annual conference plan for responding to the media
- how you handle the media.

To learn more about developing a plan, work with a public relations communicator in your church or community or contact the communicator who works for your annual conference. They will advise you on how to provide facts to the media to support your congregation and how to write an appropriate message. Remember, the quicker the facts are made known, the quicker the rumors will die.

## Giving Feedback: Communication Skills for Measuring Ministry

The S/PPRC has primary responsibility to work with staff so that the congregation's mission and vision are fulfilled. This includes providing feedback to the congregation, the staff, and the district superintendent about the way staff and congregation work together. Assessment of ministry should raise awareness of mission and vision for both the congregation and the staff. Assessment tools and examples are listed among the resources at the end of this Guideline.

Begin the measurement with consideration of the:
- place where ministry takes place—the community, the church and its history, people and their history.
- mission/vision statements of the congregation and charge conference goals.
- tasks or job description of the staff person being assessed.
- performance of the individual. What kind of results does the individual obtain? What results do we desire and expect? How can we help?.
- gifts, skills, and ability of the individual. What qualities are present, and which ones are lacking? How can we help by matching our needs with the available skills? Perhaps rewriting the job description will help.
- team-ministry approach. How can more members become team members to share the load?

## Mediation Skills: Resolving Problems

Conflict is simply two different ideas in the same place at the same time. Conflict is normal in communities and families. *The important part of conflict management is bringing those conflicts into the open where they can be clarified.*

Good communication is a key for mediating conflict. Careful listening builds understanding by all the people who are involved. Once understanding is achieved, begin to work with one another to resolve the conflict. If the conflict is handled properly, a strengthened church can result. Know when to ask for help. Earlier is better! See suggestions in the Resources list.

## A Story of Conflict in a Congregation

The December charge conference erupted at Clearview United Methodist Church when the finance committee proposed a budget for a new staff position. When questions were raised, the people learned that the S/PPRC had recommended a new position for a family center director. Others at the meeting thought the new position should be focused on youth ministry; others wanted a music position. The result was that the budget for the position was defeated!

In January, the church council recognized that the congregation had several different visions for ministry, which caused the conflict. This healthy congregation recognized the conflict and took steps to increase communication. They named a Vision Task Force and engaged a church consultant to help them bring their vision into sharper focus. Clearly the Spirit was moving among the people of Clearview. The task force members surveyed the congregation and community in order to acknowledge and address the different opinions expressed at charge conference. The council and task force used their gathered information as one means to seek God's guidance. Vital, healthy congregations communicate openly and recognize conflict as an opportunity to listen deeply for God's direction.

# Ministers Together

The apostle Paul, writing to the church in Rome (Romans 12:4-8) and to us, stated that *we are all members of the body of Christ*. Each of us has different gifts that God can use, and we are all ministers to God's saving grace. Some are ordained to preach, to teach the Word of God, to administer the sacraments of baptism and the Lord's Supper, and to lead the church in ministries in the world.

Each Christian is a baptized minister, and we minister to those around us. It may be the service organization we belong to, or the baseball team, or our family, or the school. Through our connectional system and our individual baptisms, we reach out beyond our local church. Jesus told the disciples and us to "Go therefore and make disciples of all nations" (Matthew 28:19). Each of us needs to minister to all people so they may be brought into full relationship with Christ's Body.

The United Methodist Church recognizes several forms of ministry by ordaining, consecrating, certifying, licensing, and commissioning individuals. These are deacons, elders, local pastors, diaconal ministers, deaconesses, missionaries, and certified personnel. All of these people have committed themselves to specialized training for ministry. They, along with the laity in the local congregation, make up the ministry of the Church. You may not have all of these forms of ministry present in your congregation. Which do you have?

The S/PPRC models how a group talks about its understanding of ministry and how laypeople and clergy minister together. For example read Mark 2:1-12 and discuss "ministry." Complete the following thoughts:

1. I was ministering to someone when . . . .
2. Someone ministered to me when . . . .
3. The spiritual gift that I see in you (name of each committee member) is . . . .
4. I believe God is leading me into a ministry of . . . .
5. The support I can give others who minister is . . . .
6. I would like this committee to help me develop my faith by . . . .
7. Our committee's ministry is . . . .

The task of the S/PPRC calls for balancing the mission of the church with the commitment, skills, and talents of those in ministry. The committee needs to assign tasks to those who have the skills necessary to do the task. Consider the lay members as well as the pastor(s) for these tasks. For example, you may find members who are skilled at making hospital calls and will offer a ministry to those hospitalized. When we affirm gifts of the laity and of the clergy and weave them together, we are truly ministers together.

# Support for the Clergy and Staff

Supporting the staff is more than saying, "Hello, how are you?" on Sunday morning. It is more than saying, "Thank you" when a staff member has performed a job. *Support is building relationships between people; it is getting to know one another so that you know when something is bothering the other person even when nothing is said.*

Stress and pressure sap the strength of church staff as much as they drain the strength of other people. The S/PPRC has an important role supporting the morale of the staff and providing positive, helpful feedback. Pastors need friendly advisers: people to suggest how best to handle some of the joys, concerns, and issues of the parish. This function of counsel determines, in large measure, the degree to which the shared vision can be achieved. *The S/PPRC members are chosen because they have the ability, by way of the Holy Spirit, to discern what the pastor (and staff) need, what the church needs, and how to bring these needs together for ministry.* Possessing the information that the S/PPRC can provide is essential to developing and meeting the mission and ministry direction of the congregation and pastor.

## Specific Support

Each year the committee needs to review salary and non-salary support for each staff member. Remember that your annual conference sets minimum salary recommendations for ordained ministers. Ask the lay member of the annual conference from your church to discuss the action taken by the conference with the committee before the committee makes compensation recommendations for the coming fiscal year.

For other staff members, assign a member of the committee to contact other churches of a similar size in your vicinity to discover their salary scale for the same services. This will help you determine equitable salary for your lay staff.

Other aspects of support for all employees include determining:
1. working conditions, including working space, office helpers (volunteers), equipment, and hours.
2. travel expenses, including car or car allowance, pulpit supply, annual conference session-attendance allowance, continuing education for both clergy and employed staff, moving expenses, and so forth.
3. compensation for the pastoral staff, including salary, housing, utilities, and other benefits mentioned above. The *Book of Discipline* requires provision of adequate housing for pastors, and housing is not considered part of compensation (although there are federal tax implications). Determine fringe benefits for all employees to include Social Security,

Worker's Compensation, insurance, opportunity for the pension program, and vacation allowances. Some conferences have vacation policies for clergy.

Your committee's recommendations go to the church council for its consideration. That report may be as you recommended, or it may differ. If it differs, the S/PPRC has the right and the responsibility to advise the council or the charge conference of its recommendations and the reasoning behind that decision. However, the charge conference has the final decision on salary matters.

## Continuing Education and Spiritual Formation

If individuals are to be effective in their ministry, they must have opportunities to expand their knowledge and skills through continuing education and their identity and relationship with God through spiritual formation. Continuing education is not just for the ordained staff but for other church employees as well.

Ordained elders and deacons are required to report at charge conference on their continuing education and spiritual formation of the past year and plans for the new year. Many churches provide continuing education funds as part of the pastoral ministry for this purpose. Many annual conferences have standards, requirements, and guidelines for continuing education. Check your annual conference journal for these. Talk with the clergy staff about a plan for meeting, or exceeding, these standards and guidelines.

If your pastor's plan calls for additional financial aid, it may be possible to obtain it from the Ministerial Education Fund (MEF). One-fourth of this fund is retained in each annual conference and is administered by the conference board of ordained ministry for theological education, enlistment, and continuing education. The MEF is an apportioned fund. Your committee should tell the congregation about this fund and support 100 percent remittance to the MEF.

Talk with other staff people about their own continuing education. Church secretaries and building maintenance staff can benefit by taking advantage of seminars offered in your own community or nearby communities. Many annual conferences provide workshops for secretaries, Christian educators, youth ministers, and directors of music, choir directors, and organists. Professional organizations for United Methodists provide resources and workshops for musicians, educators, youth ministers, church secretaries, and church administrators.

Many areas for possible growth and learning are enumerated in the *Book of Discipline,* such as pulpit supply, visitations, and so forth. The pastor is allowed to take one week each year and one month during one year of each quadrennium for continuing education and spiritual formation. This is not a vacation but a time of learning that will enhance the ministry of the pastor and the congregation. Furthermore, a pastor who has held a full-time appointment for at least six years is permitted to request an educational leave of up to six months while continuing to hold an appointment. The pastor will need to have a careful discussion with the committee and the district superintendent if he or she is seeking such a plan. One part of such a plan is determining alternative pastoral leadership while the leave is in effect and the financial obligations that may go along with that leadership.

# The S/PPRC in Ministry With Ordained, Appointed Staff

There are four ongoing functions for the Staff/Pastor-Parish Relations Committee with ordained elders and deacons who are members of the annual conference and appointed to your church by the bishop. These four functions are interpretation, assessing effectiveness, providing feedback, and consulting with the district superintendent. Remember, it is not the job of the S/PPRC to define the mission and vision. Rather, the S/PPRC communicates and interprets to staff and congregation so that ministry is aligned with mission.

## Interpretation

This continued communication and interpretation of the local church's mission and vision is one of the most important roles of the S/PPRC. The S/PPRC provides employed leaders with consistent reminders of the common aim and direction of ministry to church members, staff, and community. When the members take on this task sufficiently, growth in ministry is the natural result.

The S/PPRC tells the congregation about the forms of ministry in The United Methodist Church: lay ministry, licensed ministry, certified ministry, and ordained ministry, such as deacon and elder. The S/PPRC also tells the congregation about the United Methodist understanding of education and credentialing for clergy, about the Ministerial Education Fund, and about the open itinerancy of The United Methodist Church. Information in the *Book of Discipline* will help you with this important communication. The General Board of Higher Education and Ministry provides brochures, posters, videos, and staff to assist.

In order to interpret ministry to the congregation, the S/PPRC members themselves must be growing in the knowledge and love of God and in their understanding of the local church ministry. Regular worship attendance, church school or Bible study, and regular systematic giving are essential if members are to bring integrity to the interpretive function of this ministry. When this is done, the members articulate well the local church vision, not only because they know it but also because they live it! Living within the context of the mission and vision allows the members to speak as informed, faithful proponents about what God has given to the pastor and the people together.

# Assessing Effectiveness and Providing Feedback

Measuring ministerial competence is essential to the continued growth and development of the ordained staff, the lay staff, and the local church. *Thus, the spiritual and theological value of assessment must not only be stressed, it must also be featured.* The Staff/Pastor-Parish Relations Committee has the opportunity to encourage, develop, and improve the ministry of the church in untold ways when it measures the effectiveness of the local church and the staff. This process provides opportunity for the S/PPRC to help the staff focus on priority tasks for the mission and vision of the congregation. If the S/PPRC has a legal or ethical concern related to an appointed leader, it must consult with the district superintendent.

See "Giving Feedback: Communication Skills for Measuring Ministry" (page 18) and the Resources list at the end of this booklet for help with assessment.

Assessing the pastor(s) and the local church should be done in a context of Christian community. The purpose of appraisal is to build up the body of Christ. It is therefore to be exercised in a spirit of love and care. Committee members should realize that the growth and development of the congregation are dependent upon a loving yet earnest assessment, not only of the pastor but also of the congregation and how the church is bringing Good News effectively to your unique setting. The S/PPRC needs to develop a process that includes on-going self-assessment, group assessment, feedback, recommendations for growth, and plans for implementing recommendations.

The S/PPRC is responsible for the assessment of lay staff as well as appointed clergy. The previous paragraph describes the context and has suggestions. The committee also functions to consider when changes are needed in the number of paid personnel. This always happens within the vision/mission context of the local church.

The *Book of Discipline* calls for the S/PPRC to provide assessment annually for the pastor's and staff's use in an effective, ongoing ministry and for identifying continuing education needs and plans (¶259.2f[3]). Your conference board of ordained ministry and cabinet has prepared the criteria, processes, and training for evaluation and continuing education. Check with them for their guidance.

*The assessment process should be a dialogue with the individual being evaluated and the group or person making the assessment. The pastor and the staff should agree upon which method will be used for measurement. Completing these statements is a good start:*

1. I (or we) have grown in this congregation because . . . .
2. Strengths and satisfying experiences our pastor has had are . . . .
3. Helpful things our staff people have done (or tried to do) were . . . .
4. Areas for growth in this staff person are . . . .
5. Our committee is showing its support by . . . .

The content of those sessions needs to be from your own experiences and feelings—not what someone else has said. Be honest and straightforward as you share your feelings, but be tactful and diplomatic. Always begin with the strengths and elaborate on them. Remember the different gifts given to each of us by God.

## Annual Assessment

As was pointed out earlier, the committee needs to agree with the pastor and the staff about the time and procedures for annual assessment of ministry. This could be called an "assessment covenant." It could be a celebration of the gifts and work of the pastor/staff. See suggestions for assessment in the sections "Giving Feedback: Communication Skills for Measuring Ministry" (page 18) and "Assessing Effectiveness and Providing Feedback" (page 25), and in the Resources list.

Ask each person for a report of their accomplishments, and celebrate them. In addition, encourage each person to ask for help, as necessary, to accomplish those goals. For instance, the church office staff may need special training to be able to use new equipment to its full potential; the S/PPRC should be prepared to help them obtain this training as continuing education. Church Christian education staff may need training to use video, CD-DVD, or other equipment. Solicit the needs of the staff and the pastor and find ways to fill those needs.

Review the goals set for the pastor/staff. Be sure to include those that were set by the charge or church conference and by what the *Book of Discipline* says about the nature and function of pastoral ministry.

Find out what differences there are between assumptions about the church and actual facts. For instance, how many hours are available each week for the different areas of ministry? (Number of people multiplied by hours equals total hours.) What financial resources are available for the different areas of ministry? Help staff and congregation understand the priorities set for the pastoral work, administrative tasks, and building maintenance.

Review with the staff the plan for division of responsibilities for the various areas of ministry. Should these responsibilities stay the same or be shifted? If a change is needed, to whom will added responsibilities go and to what effect?

# Consulting With the District Superintendent

There are times when pastoral change is necessary. New discernment in the call of the clergyperson, appointment needs of the annual conference, and needs of the local church are all reasons why pastoral change may be initiated. When this occurs, the S/PPRC conveys the local church's needs and desires to the district superintendent. The district superintendent utilizes knowledge of the local church's vision and mission to represent the church in the appointive process. (This is described in the *Book of Discipline,* ¶¶432-433.)

The United Methodist connectional system allows for a pooling of clergy gifts and grace, making available a wide array of clergy for service. This clergy pool is deployed for the annual conference by the bishop and the cabinet.

This cooperative system allows United Methodists to retain qualified clergy for local churches on a continual basis. The S/PPRC is responsible for modeling and ensuring fairness, justice, and appreciation for those who facilitate God's work in the name of the church. An effective and responsible Staff/Pastor-Parish Relations Committee moves the local church toward attaining its God-given vision and mission.

For this system to function well the S/PPRC needs to know the vision and mission of the church. This knowledge helps the committee keep the present pastor informed about needed directions, or it helps the bishop and the cabinet identify the gifts and grace needed for the next spiritual leader of the congregation. Clarity in consultation leads to the best possible match for clergy leadership.

# Other Issues of Ministry With Ordained, Appointed Staff

The Staff/Pastor-Parish Relations Committee is the team in the local church that has primary responsibility for managing relationships when there are staff changes. In The United Methodist Church, the ordained staff is appointed to serve until the bishop reappoints them, and the appointment process is considered once a year. Each year (usually in late winter), after the assessment of the congregation and pastor, the S/PPRC and the district superintendent consult about clergy leadership for the following year.

When there is a change in ministerial leadership, some members of the congregation will be disappointed to see the former pastor leave. It is easy to become attached to a person who has been close to families in times of crisis and celebration. It is hard to say goodbye. When leaving, the pastor should express thanks for accomplishments and for having been able to help the congregation dream about the future.

### Saying Goodbye to Clergy and Staff

The consultation process between the S/PPRC and district superintendent is confidential. (See comments in "Your First Meeting," page 14.) Talk with the district superintendent about the appropriate time to request a change. Remember that the bishop makes the final appointment.

When the bishop announces an appointment change, plan opportunities to celebrate the ministry of the pastor and congregation during your life together. The S/PPRC can model for the congregation a healthy acceptance of and the process for grieving the loss of a pastor (and his or her family). Work through feelings of anger, hurt, loss, and fear of failure. Do not dump previous feelings and frustrations on the new pastor; let her or him begin with a clean slate.

Ask your district superintendent about a conference policy related to pastors returning to do weddings, funerals, or visitations. Generally these life passages should be shared between the congregation and the new pastor. If there is any difficulty, appeal to the district superintendent for help.

The S/PPRC can provide opportunities for congregational members to write letters and make other expressions of appreciation to the exiting pastor. *The United Methodist Book of Worship* has a service of farewell for a pastor.

The S/PPRC needs to be alert to avoiding gossip (as opposed to facts) about the incoming pastor. Use good listening and communication skills.

## First-time Pastors

Some congregations will have the opportunity to be the first charge for a pastor. You can help the new pastor by setting two or three goals as priorities to help the pastor learn to allocate time. The S/PPRC needs to take the lead to check with the pastor on how well the goals are being met. Some congregations provide the first appointment for a series of pastors. These congregations may understand that their mission and ministry is to nurture good pastors for a lifetime of service.

## So, a New Pastor Is Coming

The United Methodist Church has an open itinerancy system for providing pastoral leadership. From the beginning, when pastors traveled their circuits on horseback, our church has practiced this traveling ministry. The bishop and the cabinet work with the S/PPRC to appoint pastors. *We do not "call" them.* The bishop and cabinet examine the church and attempt to make a match, providing a pastor who has the skills and training to meet the needs and goals of the local church. Sometimes the local church and the bishop and cabinet will not agree. But, as a connectional church, experience has shown that the system works!

One of the reasons it works is the relationship that develops between the church and the district superintendent. A unique form of trust develops as the district superintendent comes to know the congregation—its needs, goals, and concerns. Trust develops when the S/PPRC has continuous, close consultation with the superintendent. Pastoral appointments are to be nondiscriminatory— made without regard to race, ethnic origin, gender, or age. The S/PPRC should discuss this openly with the congregation prior to a pastoral change and not wait until the midst of a change.

Sometimes the district superintendent is able to visit each church only once a year, to hold the charge/church conference. Put the district superintendent on the mailing list for the parish newsletter, letters that go out to the membership, and even the Sunday bulletins. You may want to invite him or her to come to a meeting with the committee to share times of rejoicing at meeting goals or celebrating events such as anniversaries. Open lines of communication, again, are the key.

Remember that the work of the S/PPRC is confidential. Check with the district superintendent about when to announce the appointment of a new elder and deacon. Consideration must be given to the current leaders and to the other congregation where leaders are currently serving. *Remember that appointments are official only when the bishop announces them!*

Members of the S/PPRC should encourage the congregation to attend worship on the new pastor's first Sunday. The S/PPRC chair and committee introduce the new staff to the new community. In all sizes of communities, new pastors will have a quicker and smoother transition if they know who is influential in the community, the taboos in the community, community traditions and celebrations, community policies, and the practices and agencies available for social services. The S/PPRC tells the congregation and the community the pastor's preferences about civic involvement as well as the pastor's unique gifts for church and civic leadership.

Each pastor who goes to a new appointment may be grieving over leaving the prior one, and the new congregation needs to be aware of this. Pastors need time to get acquainted in the new community at large as well as with the congregation. Allot time for personal, spiritual, and family needs. It takes time for the congregation to discover the qualities of leadership that the new pastor brings.

Each time a pastor or other staff member begins a new appointment, a church has an opportunity for members to become personally involved in ministry. The gifts of all the people of God, lay and clergy, form the identity, the mission, and the ministry of the church. *Remember (and help others remember) that the pastor's family is not an extension of the pastor.* Share clear policies with the congregation and the pastor's family about the care of the parsonage (if there is one) and the privacy issues for the family living in the parsonage or elsewhere.

You should not be surprised if your new minister is a woman or a member of an ethnic group different from the majority of the congregation. Welcome this new minister to the congregation and community. The S/PPRC members need to be the leaders who call the congregation to hospitality and support of the new pastor. The S/PPRC is charged with setting the tone of acceptance, cooperation, and support of the new pastor—whatever the race, ethnicity, gender, or age. Affirm the gifts of the Holy Spirit given to all God's people and celebrate our oneness in God.

### So, a New Deacon Is Coming
The heart of Christian ministry is Christ's ministry of outreaching love. The ordained deacon in full connection leads God's people in living as Christian disciples in the community of their daily lives. Deacons in full connection may have a primary appointment in your congregation and lead in equipping people for ministry through Christian education, music, parish nursing, professional counseling, administration, and other ministries. A deacon in full connection may work in the community and have a secondary appoint-

ment to your church. The S/PPRC has responsibility for all ordained clergy appointed to the church, whether it is a primary or secondary appointment. Initiate conversations with both deacons and elders related to your church who have primary appointments beyond the congregation to learn about their ministry and to help the congregation understand how the congregation's ministry is extended through their work in the world.

The S/PPRC tells the congregation and the community about the ministry of the deacon. Affirm the gifts of the Holy Spirit in the ministry of the deacon. Celebrate opportunities for congregational service in the world and new forms of ministry to carry Christ's ministry of love and service to the world. See "Community" page 36.

### Secondary Appointment of a Deacon

Increasingly, deacons are appointed by a bishop to an agency, a school, a social service provider, a health care setting, or some other setting where the deacon carries the love of the church into the world. These deacons have a primary appointment, salary support, and assessment outside the local church. Through ordination, they are accountable to a charge conference, which is called a secondary appointment. They relate to the S/PPRC at their secondary appointment. The S/PPRC interprets the ministry of the deacon to the congregation and mission of the congregation to the deacon. The S/PPRC assists the deacon to incorporate his or her skills and gifts to further the ministry of the congregation, while recognizing the deacon's primary appointment is outside the congregation.

# The S/PPRC in Ministry With Non-Appointed, Lay Staff

Churches of all sizes hire lay staff, even if that means a musician to help with worship, a custodian, or a part-time secretary or youth minister. Churches are not exempt from federal laws related to hiring practices. Federal laws related to church employee relations are summarized and updated at http://www.gbod.org/congregational. Click the links to SPRC. You must comply with state and local laws as well. Guidance for legal and ethical practices is found in *Safe Sanctuaries,* listed in the Resources pages.

As with appointed staff, there are many ways to support all of the staff. Build relationships with all people, getting to know each other. Assist the staff to build working relationships by encouraging them to take work breaks together, to celebrate special days together, and to learn new skills together.

Help the congregation understand that they need to inform the staff when someone in the congregation is hospitalized or when someone needs a visit. Sometimes members feel hurt or slighted by the staff when the problem can be solved by better communication.

The S/PPRC is responsible for assessing the effectiveness of all staff and providing feedback for growth and development. The suggestions earlier in this guideline should be adapted for lay staff.

The S/PPRC can enhance the ministry of your congregation by alleviating stress on the pastor and the staff. Make sure your staff gets positive feedback, and monitor the quality of life of the pastor, staff members, and their families. Encourage them to have regular time off.

All personnel records for lay employees must be kept in a safe, locked location and access to all records should be limited to people who "need to know." Check with a lawyer if you have questions.

## Specific Support

Annually review salary and non-salary support for every staff member. For lay staff members, assign a member of the committee to contact other churches in your vicinity to discover their salary scale for such services. This will help you determine equitable salary for all your staff.

Other aspects of support for all employees are listed in this Guideline under the section on clergy "Specific Support." For lay employees, give special attention to:

1. working conditions, including working space, procedures with office helpers (volunteers), equipment, and hours. Generally, background checks are required for all employees.
2. continuing education for all staff (time and costs). Remember to include continuing education for job skills, working together, and legal and ethical responsibilities.
3. benefits, including worker's compensation, insurance, pension payments, and social security.

Your committee's recommendations go to the finance committee for its consideration. They will make their report to the church council. That report may be as you recommended, or it may differ. If it differs, the S/PPRC has the right and responsibility to advise the council or the charge conference of its recommendations and the reasoning behind that decision. However, the charge conference has the final decision on salary matters.

## Personnel Committee of the S/PPRC

The S/PPRC should consider the need for a personnel committee. This is especially true if yours is a large church with several employees. The personnel committee would have the responsibility of recommending personnel policies, including hiring, supervising, and firing, as well as financial compensation. Job descriptions, line of supervision, and job assessment would all be handled by the personnel committee, which would report to and seek approval from the S/PPRC. A very large church may have a staff person who oversees personnel and relates to S/PPRC.

When hiring lay staff, remember to develop and post a job description, conduct background checks of candidates under serious consideration, contact references of applicants, and meet legal requirements. See Resources for help.

The *Book of Discipline* says that the committee and the pastor shall recommend to the church council in a written statement the policy and procedures regarding the process for hiring, evaluating, promoting, retiring, and dismissing staff personnel who are not subject to episcopal appointment as ordained clergy (¶259.2f[10]). All this must be done in consultation with the pastor-in-charge and with due process. A written personnel policy will help you and the committee through the maze of relationships that too frequently cause hard feelings that can last for many years.

These policies and procedures also need to comply with the laws of the state and any annual conference rules regarding employment by local churches. Check with your district superintendent or your conference staff for advice.

## A Checklist for Policy and Procedures for Hiring Lay Staff

___ 1. Expectation of job descriptions
___ 2. Recruiting, advertising process
___ 3. Training qualifications and certification standards
___ 4. Hiring (need for resume, references, background check, and interviews)
___ 5. Statement regarding sexual harassment and misconduct
___ 6. Evaluation procedures
___ 7. Promotion procedures
___ 8. Termination procedures
___ 9. Grievance procedures
___10. Affirmative action procedures
___11. Health and life insurance
___12. Pension benefits
___13. Relationship between the employee, the supervisor, and the committee

When you have finished your statements, present them to the church council for approval. Provide copies prior to the meeting. Recommend that policies require action at two separate meetings before they take effect. A sample church policy is available at http://www.gbod.org/congregational. Click the link to S/PPRC.

# Relating to the Congregation

The S/PPRC has the important task of communicating the work of the staff to the congregation and communicating feedback from the congregation to the staff. The S/PPRC works with other congregational leaders to initiate ongoing discussion about the congregation's vision and goals, mission, and ministry. This is done in concert with the lay leader, the church council, and others. Discussion—including active listening—of the congregation's mission, vision, and goals will help the S/PPRC guide and support the ordained and lay staff. Annually, you will need to consider the following questions with the congregation, with other congregational leaders and staff.

1. What are the goals of this congregation for ministry?
2. What is the neighborhood context where ministry takes place?
3. What is the job description and position of all the staff? How well is the job being done based on mutually understood criteria?
4. How can we help match our needs with the available skills? Will rewriting the job description help? Can the gifts of members of the congregation be used more effectively to supplement and enhance staff?
5. How can more members become team members to share the load?

# Committees, Community, and Congregation

## Committees

Consult with other chairpeople or administrators who relate to staff people (for example, trustees with the custodian; worship with musicians and worship leaders; education with the director of Christian education, director of youth ministries, and daycare teachers). These consultations will cover issues raised in the section "Support for the Clergy and Staff," pages 18. As indicated earlier, your committee's recommendations for staff salaries and benefits go to the finance committee for its consideration.

The committee, S/PPRC, and staff should agree on what to report to the congregation and to the church council. Ask the pastor(s) and employed lay staff to evaluate the effectiveness of the S/PPRC work with staff committees. Review annually the responsibilities assigned and see what has worked, as well as what needs to be improved and ways that can be done.

# Community

The S/PPRC can review with staff the need to lead ministry into the world outside the church. The community is where people live out their daily lives. In the community, the lonely, the hurt, and the hungry, the powerful, the rich, the poor, and those in between are waiting to experience the transforming power of God's love. The church's mission in every age has involved developing disciples and sending them into their community, into the world. Raise questions with staff and lay volunteers about ways they equip the congregation for this ministry.

Recall, too, that many deacons are called first to a ministry in the community rather than to a specific local church. (See page 26.) Jesus models for us a ministry of reaching out to people with sensitivity to their needs and concerns, their hopes and dreams. Reaching out to the community and receiving people into the faith family means seeking out and accepting people just as they are. Seeking out and welcoming people who may be different from those people already members of the congregation, or who may have different physical or spiritual needs, are at times frightening and difficult tasks. This is one of the greatest challenges for Christian disciples. The S/PPRC can help staff clarify the vision of the congregation for following the Great Commission. It is very important for the S/PPRC to support the staff when the congregation is challenged by the staff to reach out.

# Congregation

Encouraging people in their relationship to God and inviting them to commitment in Jesus Christ involves providing opportunities through which they can find God, including worship, study of the Scripture, and sharing their faith stories and journeys with one another. Providing activities, events, and situations in which people can experience God's presence and come to accept God's love for them is an important function of a Christian congregation.

*Leadership for the church always comes from the laity. The heart of Christian ministry is Christ's ministry of outreaching love.* All Christians are called to the ministry of a servant in the world to serve and witness with deeds and words that heal and free. (See the *Book of Discipline,* ¶¶120—135.) The Staff/Pastor-Parish Relations Committee has a responsibility to help teach the congregation this understanding of ministry. The S/PPRC can work with the lay leader and other committees to celebrate the ministry of all Christians and to help each Christian understand his or her role as a minister of Jesus Christ.

There are some whom God calls for ordained ministry from the people of the church. The S/PPRC is charged with the responsibility of discerning those whom God has called to represent Christ's ministry in the name of the church. This discernment is done with prayer and under guidance of the Holy Spirit. The S/PPRC has responsibility for the recruitment of people who show evidence of God's claim upon them for ordained ministry, the examination of candidates for their calls from God and the evidence of gifts, and the recommendation of these candidates to the charge conference. When the charge conference votes to recommend a candidate for ordained ministry, the congregation assumes care and support of the candidate through the years of preparation for ministry. The care and support may include continued prayer by individuals and during services of worship, cards and care packages during years of education, opportunities for worship leadership, financial support, and other forms of encouragement.

Aid for this task of recruitment comes from *The Christian as Minister and the Ministry Inquiry Process* (see Resources). At least one member of the S/PPRC should be trained as a guide for the Ministry Inquiry Process. The conference board of ministry provides this training.

Enlistment and recruitment of people for ministry is of paramount importance to the growth and development of the total church. Leadership that is Spirit-led and vision-driven helps the church to tell the good news of God through Jesus Christ. In this way, the S/PPRC ministers to and through the entire United Methodist Church, not only in the present but also for years to come.

# Resources

## Resources for Pastor/Staff Parish Relations Committee

• Holy Bible (there are many translations)

• *The Book of Discipline of The United Methodist Church* (Nashville, The United Methodist Publishing House, 2004.

• *Lay Speakers Are Servant Leaders,* by Thomas R. Hawkins (Nashville: Discipleship Resources, 1999. ISBN 0-88177-254-2).

## Understanding The United Methodist Church

• *A Brief History of The United Methodist Church* (Nashville: Discipleship Resources, 1996. ISBN 0-88177-256-9).

• *A Brief Introduction to the Book of Discipline,* by Branson L. Thurston (Nashville: Discipleship Resources, 1998. ISBN 0-88177-243-7).

• *Lay Speakers Interpret to Others our United Methodist Heritage,* by Chester E. Custer (Nashville: Discipleship Resources, 2001. ISBN 0-88177-380-8).

## Job Descriptions, Legal and Ethical Responsibilities

• *The Buck Stops Here,* by Mary Logan (Nashville: Discipleship Resources, 2000. ISBN 0-88177-306-9).

• Frequently Asked Questions on clergy compensation and hiring lay employees. See Pastors and local church documents on the GCFA Web site at http://www.gcfa.org.

• *Guidelines for Developing Church Job Descriptions,* The General Board of Higher Education and Ministry, free download from http://www.gbhem.org/ResourceLibrary/HE4056.pdf.

• *Guidelines for Developing Church Personnel Policies,* The General Board of Higher Education and Ministry, free download from http://www.gbhem.org/ResourceLibrary/4055.pdf.

• *Guidelines for the Professional Staff-Pastor/Staff Relations Committee When Interviewing,* The General Board of Higher Education and Ministry, free download from http://www.gbhem.org/ResourceLibrary/he4050.pdf.

• *Sample Local Church Policy Manual,* The General Board of Discipleship, free download from  http://www.gbod.org/congregational.

• *Ministry of Christian Education and Formation: A Practical Guide for Your Congregation* (Nashville: Discipleship Resources, 2003. ISBN 0-88177-395-6). See chapter 8, "Creating Job Descriptions."

• *Policy for a Congregation on Sexual Misconduct,* sample available at http://www.gcfa.org. Click on the "A-Z Listing," then on S for the sexual misconduct document. The sample is an embedded link within the article.

- *Safe Sanctuaries,* by Joy Thornburg Melton (Nashville: Discipleship Resources, 1998. ISBN 0-88177-220-8).

- *Safe Sanctuaries for Youth,* by Joy Thornburg Melton (Nashville: Discipleship Resources, 2003. ISBN 0-88177-404-9).

## Leading Meetings, Planning the Work

- *Behavioral Covenants in Congregations: A Handbook for Honoring Differences,* by Gilbert R. Rendle (Bethesda: Alban Institute, 1998. ISBN 1566992095).

- *Lay Speakers Lead Small Groups,* by Thomas R. Hawkins (Nashville: Discipleship Resources, 2001. ISBN 0-88177-315-8).

- *Spiritual Preparation for Christian Leadership,* by E. Glenn Hinson (Nashville: Upper Room Books, 1999. ISBN 0-8358-0888-2).

- *What Every Leader Needs to Know* series (Nashville: Discipleship Resources, 2004.

## Building Skills

- *How Shall They Hear? A Handbook for Religion Communicators* (Dallas: UMR Communications, ISBN 0-9679757-0-0).
  Go to http://www.religioncommunicators.org/handbook.html for an order form. No-nonsense information about every aspect of communications from developing a mission statement to choosing the appropriate media for a particular message.

## Celebration of Staff Work

- *The United Methodist Book of Worship* (Nashville: Abingdon Press, 1992. ISBN 0-687-03572-4). See especially Section VII, "Occasional Services" and Section IX "Services Relating to Congregations and Buildings."

## Identifying Ministers in the Congregation

- *The Christian as Minister,* by Robert Kohler (Nashville: Board of Higher Education and Ministry, 2001. ISBN X804294).

- *First Steps to Ministry* (Video and Guide) (Nashville: Board of Higher Education and Ministry). Call 615-340-7389 to request these resources.

- *Ministry Inquiry Process* (Video) (Nashville: Board of Higher Education and Ministry). Call 615-340-7389 to request these resources.

- *Ministry Inquiry Process* (Guidebook) (Nashville: Board of Higher Education and Ministry, 2000. ISBN X816771).

**Mediation, Resolving Problems**

• Articles, information on mediation centers and services, and congregational study "Engage Conflict Well" are available through http://www.justpeaceumc.org/

• *From Stuck to Unstuck,* by Kenneth A. Halstead (Bethesda: The Alban Institute. ISBN 1-56699-203-6).

• *Making Peace with Conflict: Practical Skills for Conflict Transformation,* edited by Carolyn Schrock-Shenk and Lawrence Ressler (Scottdale, PA: Herald Press, 1999. ISBN 0-8361-9127-7).

• *Managing Church Conflicts,* by Hugh F. Halverstadt (Louisville: Westminster/John Knox Press, 1991. ISBN: 0-664-25185-4).

• *Managing Transitions: Making the Most of Change,* by William Bridges (Cambridge, Mass.: Perseus Publishing, 2003. ISBN 0-7382-0824-8).